T0381146

AGE

OF

JUSTICE

Volume I

By
W.D. Palmer

© 2020 W. D. Palmer. All rights reserved.

No part of this book may be reproduced, stored in a retrieval system, or transmitted by any means without the written permission of the author.

AuthorHouse™
1663 Liberty Drive
Bloomington, IN 47403
www.authorhouse.com
Phone: 833-262-8899

Because of the dynamic nature of the Internet, any web addresses or links contained in this book may have changed since publication and may no longer be valid. The views expressed in this work are solely those of the author and do not necessarily reflect the views of the publisher, and the publisher hereby disclaims any responsibility for them.

Any people depicted in stock imagery provided by Getty Images are models, and such images are being used for illustrative purposes only.
Certain stock imagery © Getty Images.

This book is printed on acid-free paper.

ISBN: 978-1-6655-0661-8 (sc)
ISBN: 978-1-6655-0662-5 (e)

Print information available on the last page.

Published by AuthorHouse 10/29/2020

authorHOUSE

Walter D. Palmer Leadership School

Currently W. D. Palmer is the founder and director of the W. D. Palmer Foundation (est. 1955), a repository of information-gathering on racism in health, education, employment, housing, courts, prisons, higher education, military, government, politics, law, banking, insurance, etc.

He is also the founder of the Black People's University of Philadelphia (1955) Freedom School, which was the grassroots organizing and training center for grassroots community and political leadership in Philadelphia and nationally. These organizations were run as nonprofit unincorporated associations from 1955 until 1980, when the Palmer Foundation received its 501(c)(3) federal tax exemption status.

W. D. Palmer has also been a professor, teaching American Racism at the University of Pennsylvania since the 1960's and today he is a member of the Presidents Commission on 1619, the 400-year anniversary of African slavery in America.

Professor Palmer has been a social activist leading the fight against racial injustice for over seventy years in Philadelphia and around the nation. In 2018, Philadelphia honored him for the organizing work he did to reform the Philadelphia school system in 1967.

In 2020, Philadelphia honored him for 65 years of fighting for social justice throughout the country. In 1980, he led the fight for parental school choice which helped the Governor of Pennsylvania get a law passed in 1997, and in 2000 he created the Walter D. Palmer Leadership Charter School.

In 2005, he borrowed eleven million dollars to build a 55 thousand square-foot two story building on two acres of land in North Philadelphia, which was donated to the school by the City of Philadelphia, and because of the school's rapid growth, in 2010 he acquired the Saint Bartholomew Catholic High School, for his middle and high school.

In ten years, the school grew from three hundred elementary and middle school students, to two hundred preschoolers and over a thousand kindergarten to twelfth graders. In 2005,

W. D. Palmer commissioned a muralist to paint over four hundred pre-selected portraits on the school walls, corridors, and stairwells, with a goal to paint thirty fifteen foot murals in the gymnatorium.

Although the Walter D. Palmer Leadership School recruited "at risk children" that were from seventeen of the poorest zip codes in Philadelphia and 300 percent below poverty, the school boasted of a 95% daily attendance, 100% high school graduation, and 100% post graduate placement in four year and two year colleges, trade and technology schools, or military until the school's closing in 2015.

Property Of

Name: _____

Address: _____

_____

Phone: _____

Email: _____

Emergency Contact: _____

_____

Acknowledgement

I would like to take this time to acknowledge from the beginning of the Palmer Foundation, 1955, the many contributors who helped to gather information, organize, and write the leadership, self-development, and social awareness curriculums.

From the Palmer Foundation's inception, these contributors have been composed of community members, elementary, middle- and high-school students, as well as college student volunteers and interns, along with professional contributors.

We chose this method and process because it was consistent with our history, vision, philosophy, mission, and goals of always developing leadership in practice.

These groups, who have helped to produce our materials, are the same cohorts who over the years have helped to teach and train others as well as helped to develop a national database through which these curriculum and training materials can be distributed.

The story of the Palmer Foundation is the story of building community and leadership at the same time, and the Palmer Foundation wants to give an enthusiastic endorsement in recognition of the thousands of people who have been with us on this long and arduous journey.

We want to take this time to thank the many community leaders and people that have invited us into their communities to help them reclaim and restore the many values, properties, and people who may have been threatened with the loss of finance, property, and life, because they are the true heroes and heroines that made the Palmer Foundation the success that it has become.

Public Appeal

The Palmer Foundation is a federal 501(c)(3) organization that has spent over 65 years educating and fighting for social justice in the most underserved "at risk" communities around the country. Our goals have always been to use education for human liberation and encourage "at risk" families and children to help gather, write, produce, publish, and teach others in a similar situation.

Our mission is to disseminate our leadership, self-development, social justice, and grassroots-organizing books, manuals, and learning materials across America and around the world.

Our goals are to sell these publications or to offer them in exchange for a suggested tax-exempt donation that would allow us to continue producing our leadership training, as well as grassroots community and political organizing efforts.

Ultimately, we would like to create a satellite school as a model or prototype of the Walter D. Palmer Leadership School that could be replicated around the world.

Table of Contents

INTRODUCTION

DR. PALMER, DISTINGUISHED PROFESSOR AND LIFELONG SOCIAL CHANGE ACTIVIST, ONE DAY ENCOUNTERS A MYSTERIOUS MAN WHO SAYS HIS NAME IS *MR. JAMES*...

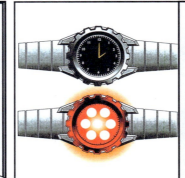

AFTER BEFRIENDING DR. PALMER, MR. JAMES MYSTERIOUSLY DISAPPEARS. BUT BEFORE HE DOES, HE LEAVES DR. PALMER HIS FAVORITE WATCH.

AS DR. PALMER DISCOVERS, THE WATCH CONTAINS A HIDDEN *POWER DIAL*, WHICH ALLOWS HIM TO TRANSFORM FROM A 75-YEAR-OLD PROFESSOR INTO A REPLICA OF HIMSELF AT AGES 20, 30, 40, AND 50 – AT DIFFERENT STAGES OF HIS STRUGGLE FOR SOCIAL CHANGE.

I AM MR. JAMES. ALTHOUGH DR. PALMER DOES NOT KNOW IT YET, MYSELF AND OTHER EXTRA-CELESTIAL *AGENTS OF AGE* HAVE BEEN OBSERVING HIS LIFELONG STRUGGLE FOR SOCIAL CHANGE. WE WANT TO SUPPORT HIS EFFORTS.

DR. PALMER RECEIVES INSTRUCTIONS THAT HE MUST RETURN THE POWER DIAL IN NO MORE THAN 25 YEARS, WHEN HE REACHES AGE 100.

IN THE MEANTIME, HE HAS FULL USE OF THE POWER DIAL'S ABILITIES, AS WELL AS A RANGE OF OTHER DEVICES AND THE HELP OF SEVERAL SUPERNATURAL CREATURES, TO AID HIM IN HIS FIGHT FOR SOCIAL CHANGE.

TOPIC DEFINITION

EACH OF THE FOLLOWING PAGES IS FOCUSED ON A PARTICULAR SOCIETAL ISSUE.

EVERY TOPIC HAS A DEFINITION, INTENDED TO PROVIDE AN OVERVIEW AND BASIC FACTS AND STATISTICS.

THE GOAL OF THESE DEFINITIONS IS TO ENCOURAGE STUDENTS TO THINK ABOUT THE ISSUES AND TO PURSUE FURTHER RESEARCH AND LEARNING.

ULTIMATELY, WE WANT YOUNG PEOPLE TO THINK CREATIVELY AND FOR THEMSELVES ABOUT HOW TO RESPOND TO THESE ISSUES.

WHERE TO TURN?

EACH OF THE FOLLOWING PAGES CONTAINS A FORM WITH THE TITLE "WHERE TO TURN?" AND BLANK SPACES FOR CONTACT INFORMATION AT CITY, STATE, COUNTY, AND NATIONAL LEVELS.

STUDENTS ARE ENCOURAGED TO RESEARCH AND FILL OUT THESE FORMS, WITH THE HELP OF THEIR PARENTS AND TEACHERS. IN THIS WAY, STUDENTS, PARENTS, AND TEACHERS WILL EDUCATE THEMSELVES AND EACH OTHER WHILE GETTING INVOLVED IN THE PROJECT.

AFTER FILLING OUT THE "WHERE TO TURN" INFORMATION ON EACH PAGE, STUDENTS WILL HAVE PERSONALIZED BOOKLETS WITH THEIR OWN THINKING AND RESEARCH INSIDE.

ALCOHOL ABUSE

DR. PALMER, DISTINGUISHED PROFESSOR AND LIFELONG SOCIAL CHANGE ACTIVIST, ENCOUNTERS A MYSTERIOUS MAN CALLED MR. JAMES. UNKNOWN TO DR. PALMER, MR. JAMES IS AN *AGENT OF AGE*. PRIOR TO HIS DISAPPEARANCE, MR. JAMES LEAVES DR. PALMER HIS WRISTWATCH.

THE WATCH, DR. PALMER DISCOVERS, CONTAINS A HIDDEN *POWER DIAL*, WHICH WILL ALLOW HIM TO TRANSFORM FROM A 75-YEAR-OLD PROFESSOR INTO A REPLICA OF HIMSELF AT AGES 20, 30, 40, AND 50. THE WATCH, ALONG WITH A RANGE OF OTHER DEVICES AND THE HELP OF SEVERAL SUPERNATURAL CREATURES, ARE MEANT TO AID HIM IN HIS FIGHT FOR SOCIAL CHANGE.

AT AGE 20, DR. PALMER WAS AN *URBAN SURVIVALIST*, AN EXPERT AT NAVIGATING IN A TOUGH ENVIRONMENT AND LOOKING OUT FOR THOSE AROUND HIM.

NOW, HE USES THE POWER DIAL TO TRANFORM INTO HIS 20-YEAR-OLD SELF TO CONTINUE FIGHTING THE CHALLENGES HE CONFRONTED THEN.

POWER DIALS ARE THE SOURCE OF AN AGENT OF AGE'S ABILITIES. THEY ACT AS LINKS TO THE *GREATNESS OF TIME*.

DR. PALMER'S POWER DIAL ENABLES HIM TO *TRAVEL THROUGH TIME*. IT ALSO TELLS TIME ANYWHERE IN THE WORLD AND PROVIDES STATS ON ANY LOCAL ENVIRONMENT.

WHERE TO TURN?

WHERE SHOULD A YOUNG PERSON FACED WITH THIS ISSUE TURN? RESEARCH AND FILL OUT THE CONTACT INFORMATION BELOW.

IN YOUR CITY...
NAME: _____
PHONE: _____
EMAIL: _____

IN YOUR STATE...
NAME: _____
PHONE: _____
EMAIL: _____

IN YOUR COUNTY...
NAME: _____
PHONE: _____
EMAIL: _____

NATION-WIDE...
NAME: _____
PHONE: _____
EMAIL: _____

ALCOHOL ABUSE

IN THE U.S., NEARLY 17 MILLION ADULTS AGED 18 AND OLDER HAVE AN ALCOHOL ABUSE DISORDER.[1] IN ADDITION, MORE THAN 7 MILLION CHILDREN LIVE IN HOUSEHOLDS WITH AT LEAST ONE PARENT WHO DRINKS TOO MUCH.[2] *ALCOHOL ABUSE* IS DEFINED AS DRINKING IN EXCESS TO THE POINT WHERE IT CAUSES THE BODY HARM AND INTERFERES WITH LIVING A HEALTHY LIFE.

ALCOHOL IS ALSO A LEADING CAUSE OF DEATH. IN THE U.S., NEARLY 88,000 PEOPLE DIE ANNUALLY FROM ALCOHOL-RELATED CAUSES (IT'S RESPONSIBLE FOR NEARLY ONE THIRD OF DRIVING FATALITIES), MAKING IT THE THIRD LEADING PREVENTABLE CAUSE OF DEATH.[3]

ANIMAL ABUSE

DR. PALMER, DISTINGUISHED PROFESSOR AND LIFELONG SOCIAL CHANGE ACTIVIST, ENCOUNTERS A MYSTERIOUS MAN CALLED MR. JAMES. UNKNOWN TO DR. PALMER, MR. JAMES IS AN **AGENT OF AGE**. PRIOR TO HIS DISAPPEARANCE, MR. JAMES LEAVES DR. PALMER HIS WRISTWATCH.

THE WATCH, DR. PALMER DISCOVERS, CONTAINS A HIDDEN **POWER DIAL**, WHICH WILL ALLOW HIM TO TRANSFORM FROM A 75-YEAR-OLD PROFESSOR INTO A REPLICA OF HIMSELF AT AGES 20, 30, 40, AND 50. THE WATCH, ALONG WITH A RANGE OF OTHER DEVICES AND THE HELP OF SEVERAL SUPERNATURAL CREATURES, ARE MEANT TO AID HIM IN HIS FIGHT FOR SOCIAL CHANGE.

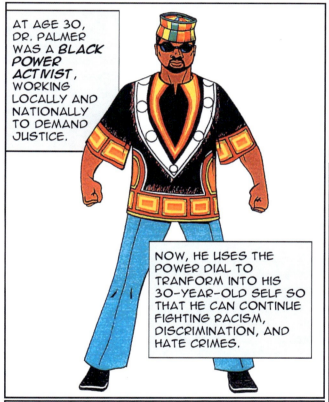

AT AGE 30, DR. PALMER WAS A **BLACK POWER ACTIVIST**, WORKING LOCALLY AND NATIONALLY TO DEMAND JUSTICE.

NOW, HE USES THE POWER DIAL TO TRANFORM INTO HIS 30-YEAR-OLD SELF SO THAT HE CAN CONTINUE FIGHTING RACISM, DISCRIMINATION, AND HATE CRIMES.

ONE OF DR. PALMER'S DEVICES IS A PAIR OF **POWER SUNGLASSES**, WHICH PROVIDE HIM WITH DISTANT DAY AND NIGHT VISION AND ALLOW HIM TO SEE THROUGH DARKNESS, WALLS, RAIN, SNOW, AND DUST STORMS!

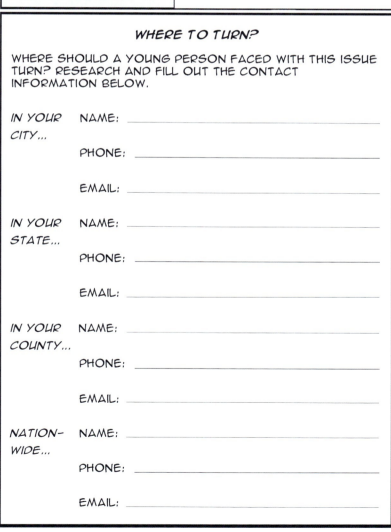

WHERE TO TURN?

WHERE SHOULD A YOUNG PERSON FACED WITH THIS ISSUE TURN? RESEARCH AND FILL OUT THE CONTACT INFORMATION BELOW.

IN YOUR CITY...

NAME: _____

PHONE: _____

EMAIL: _____

IN YOUR STATE...

NAME: _____

PHONE: _____

EMAIL: _____

IN YOUR COUNTY...

NAME: _____

PHONE: _____

EMAIL: _____

NATION-WIDE...

NAME: _____

PHONE: _____

EMAIL: _____

ANIMAL ABUSE

ANIMAL ABUSE COULD BE DELIBERATE HARM DIRECTED TOWARDS AN ANIMAL OR DEPRIVATION OF FOOD, WATER, OR SHELTER.

ANIMAL ABUSE IS VERY COMMON. IN FACT, EVERY YEAR, MORE THAN 10 MILLION ANIMALS DIE FROM ABUSE IN THE U.S. ALONE.[4]

COMMON TYPES OF ANIMAL ABUSE INCLUDE ABUSE OF PETS, ABUSE OF LIVESTOCK AND POULTRY FOR COMMERCIAL MOTIVES, AND PRACTICES SUCH AS DOGFIGHTING AND BULLFIGHTING.

IN ADDITION, INTENTIONAL CRUELTY TO ANIMALS IS STRONGLY CORRELATED WITH OTHER CRIMES, INCLUDING VIOLENCE AGAINST PEOPLE.[5]

ASBESTOS

DR. PALMER, DISTINGUISHED PROFESSOR AND LIFELONG SOCIAL CHANGE ACTIVIST, ENCOUNTERS A MYSTERIOUS MAN CALLED MR. JAMES. UNKNOWN TO DR. PALMER, MR. JAMES IS AN *AGENT OF AGE*. PRIOR TO HIS DISAPPEARANCE, MR. JAMES LEAVES DR. PALMER HIS WRISTWATCH.

THE WATCH, DR. PALMER DISCOVERS, CONTAINS A HIDDEN *POWER DIAL*, WHICH WILL ALLOW HIM TO TRANSFORM FROM A 75-YEAR-OLD PROFESSOR INTO A REPLICA OF HIMSELF AT AGES 20, 30, 40, AND 50. THE WATCH, ALONG WITH A RANGE OF OTHER DEVICES AND THE HELP OF SEVERAL SUPERNATURAL CREATURES, ARE MEANT TO AID HIM IN HIS FIGHT FOR SOCIAL CHANGE.

AT AGE 40, DR. PALMER WAS A *REVOLUTIONARY ACTIVIST*, TEACHING COMMUNITY ORGANIZING AND SUPPORTING MOVEMENTS FOR CHANGE NATIONALLY AND INTER-NATIONALLY.

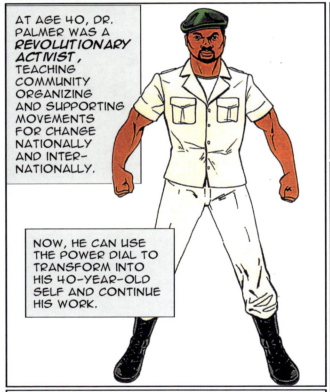

NOW, HE CAN USE THE POWER DIAL TO TRANSFORM INTO HIS 40-YEAR-OLD SELF AND CONTINUE HIS WORK.

ONE OF DR. PALMER'S DEVICES IS A *POWER HEARING DEVICE*, WHICH CAN HEAR UP TO A MILE AWAY AND TRANSLATE ANY SPOKEN LANGUAGE INTO ENGLISH!

ASBESTOS

ASBESTOS IS A NATURAL MINERAL FIBER THAT CAN BE SPUN OR WOVEN SIMILARLY TO WOOL OR COTTON. IT IS FIRE-RESISTANT AND WAS A COMMONLY USED MATERIAL FOR MANY YEARS.

HOWEVER, AIRBORNE ASBESTOS FIBERS HAVE BEEN SHOWN TO CAUSE CANCER. ASBESTOS ALSO CAUSES A LUNG DISORDER CALLED *ASBESTOSIS*.

ALTHOUGH TODAY PEOPLE KNOW THAT ASBESTOS IS DANGEROUS, IT IS STILL PRESENT IN MANY BUILDINGS – INCLUDING HOMES AND SCHOOLS – THAT WERE BUILT BEFORE THE 1980S. IN ADDITION, MANY BUILDING MATERIALS THAT CONTAIN ASBESTOS ARE NOW DETERIORATING WITH AGE, CAUSING HIGHER RISK OF EXPOSURE.

WHERE TO TURN?

WHERE SHOULD A YOUNG PERSON FACED WITH THIS ISSUE TURN? RESEARCH AND FILL OUT THE CONTACT INFORMATION BELOW. .

IN YOUR CITY...

NAME: _____

PHONE: _____

EMAIL: _____

IN YOUR STATE...

NAME: _____

PHONE: _____

EMAIL: _____

IN YOUR COUNTY...

NAME: _____

PHONE: _____

EMAIL: _____

NATION-WIDE...

NAME: _____

PHONE: _____

EMAIL: _____

BULLYING

DR. PALMER, DISTINGUISHED PROFESSOR AND LIFELONG SOCIAL CHANGE ACTIVIST, ENCOUNTERS A MYSTERIOUS MAN CALLED MR. JAMES. UNKNOWN TO DR. PALMER, MR. JAMES IS AN *AGENT OF AGE*. PRIOR TO HIS DISAPPEARANCE, MR. JAMES LEAVES DR. PALMER HIS WRISTWATCH.

THE WATCH, DR. PALMER DISCOVERS, CONTAINS A HIDDEN *POWER DIAL*, WHICH WILL ALLOW HIM TO TRANSFORM FROM A 75-YEAR-OLD PROFESSOR INTO A REPLICA OF HIMSELF AT AGES 20, 30, 40, AND 50. THE WATCH, ALONG WITH A RANGE OF OTHER DEVICES AND THE HELP OF SEVERAL SUPERNATURAL CREATURES, ARE MEANT TO AID HIM IN HIS FIGHT FOR SOCIAL CHANGE.

AT AGE 50, DR. PALMER WAS AN *ACADEMIC ACTIVIST*, ADVOCATING ON BEHALF OF STUDENTS AND TEACHING REAL-WORLD LEADERSHIP SKILLS.

NOW, HE CAN USE THE POWER DIAL TO TRANFORM INTO HIS 50-YEAR-OLD SELF AND CONTINUE THIS WORK.

AMONG DR. PALMER'S DEVICES IS A *POWER BICYCLE*, WHICH HAS 12 SPEEDS AND CAN CLIMB HILLS AND MOUNTAINS!

WHERE TO TURN?

WHERE SHOULD A YOUNG PERSON FACED WITH THIS ISSUE TURN? RESEARCH AND FILL OUT THE CONTACT INFORMATION BELOW.

IN YOUR CITY...

NAME: _____

PHONE: _____

EMAIL: _____

IN YOUR STATE...

NAME: _____

PHONE: _____

EMAIL: _____

IN YOUR COUNTY...

NAME: _____

PHONE: _____

EMAIL: _____

NATION-WIDE...

NAME: _____

PHONE: _____

EMAIL: _____

BULLYING

BULLYING IS PURPOSELY TORMENTING ANOTHER PERSON IN PHYSICAL, VERBAL, OR PSYCHOLOGICAL WAYS. IT CAN RANGE FROM HITTING, SHOVING, AND MOCKING TO DEMANDING MONEY OR POSSESSIONS.

IN THE U.S., 1 IN 5 STUDENTS AGED 12-18 HAS BEEN BULLIED IN SCHOOL,[6] AND 70% OF SCHOOL STAFF HAVE SEEN BULLYING.[7] IN ADDITION, THOUSANDS OF STUDENTS SKIP SCHOOL EACH YEAR BECAUSE THEY ARE BEING BULLIED.

COMMON TYPES OF BULLYING INCLUDE VERBAL HARASSMENT, SOCIAL HARASSMENT, PHYSICAL BULLYING, AND CYBERBULLYING.

CHILD ABUSE

DR. PALMER, DISTINGUISHED PROFESSOR AND LIFELONG SOCIAL CHANGE ACTIVIST, ENCOUNTERS A MYSTERIOUS MAN CALLED MR. JAMES. UNKNOWN TO DR. PALMER, MR. JAMES IS AN *AGENT OF AGE*. PRIOR TO HIS DISAPPEARANCE, MR. JAMES LEAVES DR. PALMER HIS WRISTWATCH.

THE WATCH, DR. PALMER DISCOVERS, CONTAINS A HIDDEN *POWER DIAL*, WHICH WILL ALLOW HIM TO TRANSFORM FROM A 75-YEAR-OLD PROFESSOR INTO A REPLICA OF HIMSELF AT AGES 20, 30, 40, AND 50. THE WATCH, ALONG WITH A RANGE OF OTHER DEVICES AND THE HELP OF SEVERAL SUPERNATURAL CREATURES, ARE MEANT TO AID HIM IN HIS FIGHT FOR SOCIAL CHANGE.

ONE OF DR. PALMER'S SUPERNATURAL ALLIES IS A GERMAN SHEPHERD GUARD DOG NAMED *WOLF*.

WOLF'S COLLAR CONTAINS A POWER DIAL SIMILAR TO THE ONE IN DR. PALMER'S WATCH. THE POWER DIAL GIVES WOLF SUPERNATURAL ABILITIES INCLUDING *IMMORTAL LIFE!*

AMONG DR. PALMER'S DEVICES IS A *POWER SONAR DEVICE*, WHICH ALLOWS HIM TO DETECT OBJECTS UNDERWATER!

WHERE TO TURN?

WHERE SHOULD A YOUNG PERSON FACED WITH THIS ISSUE TURN? RESEARCH AND FILL OUT THE CONTACT INFORMATION BELOW.

IN YOUR CITY...

NAME: _____

PHONE: _____

EMAIL: _____

IN YOUR STATE...

NAME: _____

PHONE: _____

EMAIL: _____

IN YOUR COUNTY...

NAME: _____

PHONE: _____

EMAIL: _____

NATION-WIDE...

NAME: _____

PHONE: _____

EMAIL: _____

CHILD ABUSE

CHILD ABUSE IS THE MALTREATMENT OF A CHILD BY A PARENT OR CARETAKER.

CHILD ABUSE IS VERY WIDESPREAD. IN FACT, IT IS ESTIMATED THAT 1 IN 7 CHILDREN IN THE U.S. HAS EXPERIENCED ABUSE AND/OR NEGLECT IN THE PAST YEAR.[8]

IN ADDITION, ADULT SURVIVORS OF CHILD ABUSE ARE MORE LIKELY TO EXPERIENCE MENTAL HEALTH DIFFICULTIES, INCLUDING DEPRESSION, ANXIETY, BIPOLAR DISORDER, PTSD, EATING DISORDERS, AND SUBSTANCE USE DISORDERS.[9]

CHILDREN WHO HAVE EXPERIENCED ABUSE OR NEGLECT ARE ALSO MORE LIKELY TO ENGAGE IN HIGH-RISK BEHAVIORS LIKE SMOKING, ALCOHOL AND DRUG USE, AND UNSAFE SEX.[10]

DISABILITY

DR. PALMER, DISTINGUISHED PROFESSOR AND LIFELONG SOCIAL CHANGE ACTIVIST, ENCOUNTERS A MYSTERIOUS MAN CALLED MR. JAMES. UNKNOWN TO DR. PALMER, MR. JAMES IS AN **AGENT OF AGE.** PRIOR TO HIS DISAPPEARANCE, MR. JAMES LEAVES DR. PALMER HIS WRISTWATCH.

THE WATCH, DR. PALMER DISCOVERS, CONTAINS A HIDDEN **POWER DIAL,** WHICH WILL ALLOW HIM TO TRANSFORM FROM A 75-YEAR-OLD PROFESSOR INTO A REPLICA OF HIMSELF AT AGES 20, 30, 40, AND 50. THE WATCH, ALONG WITH A RANGE OF OTHER DEVICES AND THE HELP OF SEVERAL SUPERNATURAL CREATURES, ARE MEANT TO AID HIM IN HIS FIGHT FOR SOCIAL CHANGE.

AMONG DR. PALMER'S SUPERNATURAL ALLIES ARE THE **GUARDIAN GODS** OF ALL SEVEN CONTINENTS.

NORTH AMERICA, THE **GUARDIAN OF WATER,** CAN CONTROL TIDES, BUILD GIANT WAVES, AND FLOOD RIVERS AND LAKES TO ASSIST DR. PALMER!

ONE OF DR. PALMER'S DEVICES IS A **POWER JET SKI,** WHICH CAN REACH 75-100 MPH AND CONVERT INTO A MOTORCYCLE ON LAND!

WHERE TO TURN?

WHERE SHOULD A YOUNG PERSON FACED WITH THIS ISSUE TURN? RESEARCH AND FILL OUT THE CONTACT INFORMATION BELOW.

IN YOUR CITY...

NAME: _____

PHONE: _____

EMAIL: _____

IN YOUR STATE...

NAME: _____

PHONE: _____

EMAIL: _____

IN YOUR COUNTY...

NAME: _____

PHONE: _____

EMAIL: _____

NATION-WIDE...

NAME: _____

PHONE: _____

EMAIL: _____

DISABILITY

AROUND THE WORLD, OVER 1 BILLION PEOPLE - 15% OF THE WORLD'S POPULATION - LIVE WITH SOME FORM OF **DISABILITY.**[11] IN THE U.S., 19% OF THE POPULATION HAS A DISABILITY, AND ABOUT 10% HAVE A SEVERE DISABILITY.[12]

IN SPITE OF HOW COMMON DISABILITIES ARE, PEOPLE LIVING WITH THEM FACE HIGHER RATES OF UNEMPLOYMENT, LOWER SALARIES, AND HIGHER RATES OF POVERTY THAN NON-DISABLED PEOPLE.[13] IN ADDITION, CHILDREN WITH DISABILITIES ARE LESS LIKELY TO ATTEND SCHOOL THAN NON-DISABLED CHILDREN.[14]

DISABILITY DISCRIMINATION

DR. PALMER, DISTINGUISHED PROFESSOR AND LIFELONG SOCIAL CHANGE ACTIVIST, ENCOUNTERS A MYSTERIOUS MAN CALLED MR. JAMES. UNKNOWN TO DR. PALMER, MR. JAMES IS AN *AGENT OF AGE*. PRIOR TO HIS DISAPPEARANCE, MR. JAMES LEAVES DR. PALMER HIS WRISTWATCH.

THE WATCH, DR. PALMER DISCOVERS, CONTAINS A HIDDEN *POWER DIAL*, WHICH WILL ALLOW HIM TO TRANSFORM FROM A 75-YEAR-OLD PROFESSOR INTO A REPLICA OF HIMSELF AT AGES 20, 30, 40, AND 50. THE WATCH, ALONG WITH A RANGE OF OTHER DEVICES AND THE HELP OF SEVERAL SUPERNATURAL CREATURES, ARE MEANT TO AID HIM IN HIS FIGHT FOR SOCIAL CHANGE.

AMONG DR. PALMER'S SUPERNATURAL ALLIES ARE THE *GUARDIAN GODS* OF ALL SEVEN CONTINENTS.

SOUTH AMERICA, THE *GUARDIAN OF FIRE*, CAN AID DR. PAMER BY CREATING WALLS OF FIRE AS A BLOCKADE AGAINST EVIL FORCES AND BY USING SMOKE AS A COVER OR DETERRENT FOR HIM!

ONE OF DR. PALMER'S DEVICES IS A *POWER HELICOPTER* THAT CAN REACH SPEEDS OF UP TO 400 MPH!

DISABILITY DISCRIMINATION

DISABILITY DISCRIMINATION, OR *ABLEISM*, IS THE UNEQUAL TREATMENT OF PEOPLE WITH DISABILITIES.

IN 1990, THE *AMERICANS WITH DISABILITIES ACT* WAS PASSED TO PROTECT PEOPLE WITH DISABILITIES FROM DISCRIMINATION IN JOBS.

HOWEVER, DISABLED PEOPLE STILL REPORT HIRING DISCRIMINATION AND WORKPLACE DISCRIMINATION.[15] IN ADDITION, THEY STILL FACE HIGHER UNEMPLOYMENT RATES, HIGHER POVERTY RATES, AND RECEIVE LOWER SALARIES THAN NON-DISABLED PEOPLE.[16]

WHERE TO TURN?

WHERE SHOULD A YOUNG PERSON FACED WITH THIS ISSUE TURN? RESEARCH AND FILL OUT THE CONTACT INFORMATION BELOW.

IN YOUR CITY...

NAME: _____

PHONE: _____

EMAIL: _____

IN YOUR STATE...

NAME: _____

PHONE: _____

EMAIL: _____

IN YOUR COUNTY...

NAME: _____

PHONE: _____

EMAIL: _____

NATION-WIDE...

NAME: _____

PHONE: _____

EMAIL: _____

DOMESTIC ABUSE

DR. PALMER, DISTINGUISHED PROFESSOR AND LIFELONG SOCIAL CHANGE ACTIVIST, ENCOUNTERS A MYSTERIOUS MAN CALLED MR. JAMES. UNKNOWN TO DR. PALMER, MR. JAMES IS AN **AGENT OF AGE.** PRIOR TO HIS DISAPPEARANCE, MR. JAMES LEAVES DR. PALMER HIS WRISTWATCH.

THE WATCH, DR. PALMER DISCOVERS, CONTAINS A HIDDEN **POWER DIAL,** WHICH WILL ALLOW HIM TO TRANSFORM FROM A 75-YEAR-OLD PROFESSOR INTO A REPLICA OF HIMSELF AT AGES 20, 30, 40, AND 50. THE WATCH, ALONG WITH A RANGE OF OTHER DEVICES AND THE HELP OF SEVERAL SUPERNATURAL CREATURES, ARE MEANT TO AID HIM IN HIS FIGHT FOR SOCIAL CHANGE.

AMONG DR. PALMER'S SUPERNATURAL ALLIES ARE THE **GUARDIAN GODS** OF ALL SEVEN CONTINENTS.

ASIA, THE **GUARDIAN OF THE SUN,** CAN ASSIST DR. PALMER BY INCREASING THE SUN'S HEAT OR CAUSING TEMPORARY BLINDNESS TO OVERWHELM AN ADVERSARY!

ONE OF DR. PALMER'S DEVICES IS A **POWER JETPACK,** WHICH CAN REACH SPEEDS OF 50 MPH AND TRAVEL AT UP TO 4000 FT ABOVE LAND!

WHERE TO TURN?

WHERE SHOULD A YOUNG PERSON FACED WITH THIS ISSUE TURN? RESEARCH AND FILL OUT THE CONTACT INFORMATION BELOW.

IN YOUR CITY...
NAME: _____
PHONE: _____
EMAIL: _____

IN YOUR STATE...
NAME: _____
PHONE: _____
EMAIL: _____

IN YOUR COUNTY...
NAME: _____
PHONE: _____
EMAIL: _____

NATION-WIDE...
NAME: _____
PHONE: _____
EMAIL: _____

DOMESTIC ABUSE

DOMESTIC ABUSE IS PHYSICAL, EMOTIONAL, OR SEXUAL VIOLENCE AGAINST A SPOUSE OR PARTNER.

DOMESTIC ABUSE IS VERY COMMON - IN FACT, 1 IN 4 WOMEN AND 1 IN 9 MEN EXPERIENCE SOME FORM OF ABUSE FROM THEIR PARTNERS.[17] 1 IN 10 WOMEN HAVE BEEN RAPED BY THEIR PARTNERS.[18] IN ADDITION, DOMESTIC VIOLENCE ACCOUNTS FOR 15% OF ALL VIOLENT CRIME.[19]

DOMESTIC ABUSE ALSO HAS CONSEQUENCES THAT GO BEYOND IMMEDIATE PHYSICAL DANGER. FOR INSTANCE, PEOPLE WHO HAVE EXPERIENCED DOMESTIC VIOLENCE HAVE HIGHER RATES OF DEPRESSION AND SUICIDAL BEHAVIOR THAN THOSE WHO HAVEN'T.[20]

DRUG ABUSE

DR. PALMER, DISTINGUISHED PROFESSOR AND LIFELONG SOCIAL CHANGE ACTIVIST, ENCOUNTERS A MYSTERIOUS MAN CALLED MR. JAMES. UNKNOWN TO DR. PALMER, MR. JAMES IS AN *AGENT OF AGE*. PRIOR TO HIS DISAPPEARANCE, MR. JAMES LEAVES DR. PALMER HIS WRISTWATCH.

THE WATCH, DR. PALMER DISCOVERS, CONTAINS A HIDDEN *POWER DIAL*, WHICH WILL ALLOW HIM TO TRANSFORM FROM A 75-YEAR-OLD PROFESSOR INTO A REPLICA OF HIMSELF AT AGES 20, 30, 40, AND 50. THE WATCH, ALONG WITH A RANGE OF OTHER DEVICES AND THE HELP OF SEVERAL SUPERNATURAL CREATURES, ARE MEANT TO AID HIM IN HIS FIGHT FOR SOCIAL CHANGE.

AMONG DR. PALMER'S SUPERNATURAL ALLIES ARE THE *GUARDIAN GODS* OF ALL SEVEN CONTINENTS.

AUSTRALIA, THE *GUARDIAN OF THE MOON*, CAN HAVE THE MOON RETREAT TO CAUSE DARKNESS, CONFUSION, AND A COVER FOR DR. PALMER!

ONE OF DR. PALMER'S DEVICES IS A *POWER RADAR DEVICE*, WHICH PROVIDES HIM WITH AIR SURVEILLANCE!

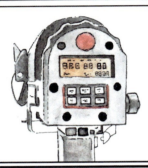

DRUG ABUSE

DRUG ABUSE IS THE USE OF ADDICTIVE DRUGS IN A WAY THAT LEADS TO INCREASED RISK OF HARM AND INABILITY TO CONTROL USE. SOME OF THE MOST COMMON CATEGORIES OF DRUGS INCLUDE:

STIMULANTS, SUCH AS METH, COCAINE, AND CRACK COCAINE, WHICH SPEED UP YOUR BODY TO MAKE YOU FEEL HIGH AND ENERGIZED.

DEPRESSANTS, SUCH AS XANAX, KLONOPIN, AND BARBITURATES, WHICH SLOW YOUR BODY DOWN.

OPIOIDS, SUCH AS OPIUM, MORPHINE, HEROIN, AND FENTANYL, WHICH RELIEVE PAIN.

HALLUCINOGENS, SUCH AS LSD AND ECSTASY/MDMA, WHICH AFFECT YOUR MOOD AND CAN MAKE YOU SEE OR HEAR THINGS THAT AREN'T REALLY THERE.

WHERE TO TURN?

WHERE SHOULD A YOUNG PERSON FACED WITH THIS ISSUE TURN? RESEARCH AND FILL OUT THE CONTACT INFORMATION BELOW.

IN YOUR CITY...
NAME: _____
PHONE: _____
EMAIL: _____

IN YOUR STATE...
NAME: _____
PHONE: _____
EMAIL: _____

IN YOUR COUNTY...
NAME: _____
PHONE: _____
EMAIL: _____

NATION-WIDE...
NAME: _____
PHONE: _____
EMAIL: _____

EDUCATION DISCRIMINATION

DR. PALMER, DISTINGUISHED PROFESSOR AND LIFELONG SOCIAL CHANGE ACTIVIST, ENCOUNTERS A MYSTERIOUS MAN CALLED MR. JAMES. UNKNOWN TO DR. PALMER, MR. JAMES IS AN *AGENT OF AGE*. PRIOR TO HIS DISAPPEARANCE, MR. JAMES LEAVES DR. PALMER HIS WRISTWATCH.

THE WATCH, DR. PALMER DISCOVERS, CONTAINS A HIDDEN *POWER DIAL*, WHICH WILL ALLOW HIM TO TRANSFORM FROM A 75-YEAR-OLD PROFESSOR INTO A REPLICA OF HIMSELF AT AGES 20, 30, 40, AND 50. THE WATCH, ALONG WITH A RANGE OF OTHER DEVICES AND THE HELP OF SEVERAL SUPERNATURAL CREATURES, ARE MEANT TO AID HIM IN HIS FIGHT FOR SOCIAL CHANGE.

AMONG DR. PALMER'S SUPERNATURAL ALLIES ARE THE *GUARDIAN GODS* OF ALL SEVEN CONTINENTS.

THE ARCTIC, *GUARDIAN OF WIND*, CAN REDIRECT WIND, STORMS, HURRICANES, AND CYCLONES TO ASSIST DR. PALMER!

ONE OF DR. PALMER'S DEVICES IS A *POWER SUBMARINE*, A HYPER-SUBMARINE THAT CAN REACH SPEEDS OF UP TO 50 MPH UNDERWATER!

EDUCATION DISCRIMINATION

EDUCATION DISCRIMINATION IS WHEN TEACHERS OR SCHOOL ADMINISTRATORS TREAT SOME STUDENTS UNFAIRLY COMPARED TO OTHERS.

DISCRIMINATION DUE TO RACE IS ESPECIALLY COMMON. FOR EXAMPLE, BLACK STUDENTS ARE 3.8 TIMES MORE LIKELY THAN WHITE STUDENTS TO RECEIVE ONE OR MORE SUSPENSIONS FROM SCHOOL.[21] STUDIES HAVE SHOWN THAT THIS IS BECAUSE BLACK STUDENTS ARE BEING PUNISHED AT A HIGHER RATE THAN OTHERS.[22]

BLACK STUDENTS ARE ALSO LESS LIKELY THAN WHITE STUDENTS TO BE SINGLED OUT IN POSITIVE WAYS. FOR INSTANCE, THEY ARE 54% LESS LIKELY TO BE RECOMMENDED FOR GIFTED-EDUCATION PROGRAMS, AFTER ADJUSTING FOR FACTORS SUCH AS STUDENTS' TEST SCORES.[23]

WHERE TO TURN?

WHERE SHOULD A YOUNG PERSON FACED WITH THIS ISSUE TURN? RESEARCH AND FILL OUT THE CONTACT INFORMATION BELOW.

IN YOUR CITY...

NAME: _____

PHONE: _____

EMAIL: _____

IN YOUR STATE...

NAME: _____

PHONE: _____

EMAIL: _____

IN YOUR COUNTY...

NAME: _____

PHONE: _____

EMAIL: _____

NATION-WIDE...

NAME: _____

PHONE: _____

EMAIL: _____

COVID-19

DR. PALMER, DISTINGUISHED PROFESSOR AND LIFELONG SOCIAL CHANGE ACTIVIST, ENCOUNTERS A MYSTERIOUS MAN CALLED MR. JAMES. UNKNOWN TO DR. PALMER, MR. JAMES IS AN *AGENT OF AGE*. PRIOR TO HIS DISAPPEARANCE, MR. JAMES LEAVES DR. PALMER HIS WRISTWATCH.

THE WATCH, DR. PALMER DISCOVERS, CONTAINS A HIDDEN *POWER DIAL*, WHICH WILL ALLOW HIM TO TRANSFORM FROM A 75-YEAR-OLD PROFESSOR INTO A REPLICA OF HIMSELF AT AGES 20, 30, 40, AND 50. THE WATCH, ALONG WITH A RANGE OF OTHER DEVICES AND THE HELP OF SEVERAL SUPERNATURAL CREATURES, ARE MEANT TO AID HIM IN HIS FIGHT FOR SOCIAL CHANGE.

AMONG DR. PALMER'S SUPERNATURAL ALLIES ARE THE *GUARDIAN GODS* OF ALL SEVEN CONTINENTS.

AFRICA, THE *GUARDIAN OF THE EARTH*, FIGHTS FOR PROTECTION OF THE ENVIRONMENT AND CAN AID DR. PALMER BY PROVIDING SHELTERS AND BLOCKADES OF EARTH!

ONE OF DR. PALMER'S DEVICES IS A *POWER MOTORCYCLE*, WHICH CAN REACH SPEEDS OF UP TO 150 MPH!

COVID-19

COVID-19 IS THE ILLNESS CAUSED BY A NEW CORONAVIRUS THAT SPREADS EASILY FROM PERSON TO PERSON.

YOU CAN BECOME INFECTED BY COMING INTO CLOSE CONTACT (WITHIN 6 FEET) OF A PERSON WHO HAS COVID-19. THE VIRUS SPREADS THROUGH RESPIRATORY DROPLETS WHEN AN INFECTED PERSON COUGHS, SNEEZES, OR TALKS. YOU MAY ALSO BECOME INFECTED BY TOUCHING A SURFACE OR OBJECT THAT HAS THE VIRUS ON IT, AND THEN TOUCHING YOUR MOUTH, NOSE, OR EYES.

IN ORDER TO PROTECT YOURSELF AND OTHERS FROM COVID-19, STAY AT HOME AS MUCH AS POSSIBLE AND AVOID CONTACT WITH OTHERS, WEAR A MASK IN PUBLIC SETTINGS, AND WASH YOUR HANDS FREQUENTLY.

WHERE TO TURN?

WHERE SHOULD A YOUNG PERSON FACED WITH THIS ISSUE TURN? RESEARCH AND FILL OUT THE CONTACT INFORMATION BELOW.

IN YOUR CITY...

NAME: _____

PHONE: _____

EMAIL: _____

IN YOUR STATE...

NAME: _____

PHONE: _____

EMAIL: _____

IN YOUR COUNTY...

NAME: _____

PHONE: _____

EMAIL: _____

NATION-WIDE...

NAME: _____

PHONE: _____

EMAIL: _____

Citations

1. Hall, Kathleen. "10 Essential Facts About Alcohol Abuse." *Everydayhealth.com*. Accessed July 28, 2020, https://www.everydayhealth.com/news/essential-facts-about-alcohol-abuse/.

2. Hall, "Alcohol Abuse."

3. Hall, "Alcohol Abuse."

4. The Humane Society of the United States. "Animal cruelty facts and stats." Accessed July 21, 2020, https://www.humanesociety.org/resources/animal-cruelty-facts-and-stats.

5. Humane Society, "Animal Cruelty."

6. StopBullying.gov. "Facts About Bullying: Statistics." Accessed August 15, 2020, https://www.stopbullying.gov/media/facts/index.html.

7. National Center for Education Statistics, "Bullying: Fast Facts." Accessed august 15, 2020, https://nces.ed.gov/fastfacts/display.asp?id=719.

8. Centers for Disease Control and Prevention. "Child Abuse & Neglect: Fast Facts." Accessed August 15, 2020, https://www.cdc.gov/violenceprevention/childabuseandneglect/fastfact.html.

9. Springer, Kristen et al. "The Long-term Health Outcomes of Childhood Abuse." *Journal of General Internal Medicine*, October 18, 2003. Accessed August 15, 2020, https://www.ncbi.nlm.nih.gov/pmc/articles/PMC1494926/.

10. Springer et al., "Childhood Abuse."

11. World Health Organization. "10 facts on disability." Accessed August 9, 2020, https://www.who.int/features/factfiles/disability/en/.

12. World Health Organization, "10 facts on disability."

13. World Health Organization, "10 facts on disability."

14. World Health Organization, "10 facts on disability."

15. World Health Organization, "10 facts on disability."

16. World Health Organization, "10 facts on disability."

17. National Coalition Against Domestic Violence. "National Statistics." Accessed August 15, 2020, https://ncadv.org/statistics.

18. National Coalition Against Domestic Violence, "National Statistics."

19. National Coalition Against Domestic Violence, "National Statistics."

20. National Coalition Against Domestic Violence, "National Statistics."

21. Weir, Kirsten. "Inequality at school." *Apa.org*, accessed August 11, 2020, https://www.apa.org/monitor/2016/11/cover-inequality-school.

22. Weir, "Inequality at school."

23. Weir, "Inequality at school."

A Brief Biography of Professor Walter Palmer

After a tumultuous juvenile life, Professor Palmer graduated from high school and was hired by the University of Pennsylvania hospital as a surgical attendant and eventually was recruited into the University of Pennsylvania School of Inhalation and Respiratory (Oxygen) Therapy.

After his certification as an inhalation and respiratory therapist, he was hired by the Children's Hospital of Philadelphia as the Director of the Department of Inhalation and Respiratory (Oxygen) Therapy, where he spent ten years helping to develop the national field of cardio-pulmonary therapy.

In 1955, Professor Palmer created the Palmer Foundation and the Black People's University of Philadelphia Freedom School and would spend the next seventy years developing leaders for social justice nationally.

Professor Palmer has also pursued further education at Temple University for Business Administration and Communications, Cheyney State University for a Teacher's Degree in History and Secondary Education. And at age 40, acquired his juris doctorate in law from Howard University.

Between 1965 and 1995, he produced and hosted radio programs on Philadelphia WDAS, Atlantic City WUSS, and WFPG Radio, in addition to Philadelphia NBC TV 10 and New Jersey Suburban Cable Television.

In 2006, he was inducted into the Philadelphia College of Physicians as a Fellow for the body of work he had done over the past 70 years, after having spent ten (1980-1990) years as a licensed financial officer teaching poor people how to overcome poverty by saving and investing three dollars per day.

During that entire period, Professor Palmer led the Civil Rights, Black Power and Afrocentric movements in Philadelphia, around the country as well as the Caribbean and West Indies.

In the 1980s to 2015, he led the school choice movement, organized a state-wide parental school choice group which collected 500,000 petitions in 1997, which were used to create a charter and cyber school law in Pennsylvania, and in 2000 the Walter D. Palmer School was named after him.

In 1962, he created a school without walls on the University of Pennsylvania's campus and became a visiting lecturer in the Schools of Medicine, Law, Education, Wharton, History, Africana Studies, Engineering, and he currently is a lecturer in the Schools of Medicine, Social Work, and Urban Studies, where he teaches courses on American racism.

In 1969, he helped the University of Pennsylvania Graduate School of Social Work students and faculty create required courses on American racism, making the University of Pennsylvania the first school in American academia to have such courses.

In 2019, Professor Palmer was appointed to the President's Commission on commemorating the four hundred year (1619) anniversary of American slavery.

Over his many years of teaching, he has received the title of Teacher Par Excellence and has amassed over 1,000 medals, trophies, plaques, certificates, and awards for participation in multiple disciplines.

W. D. Palmer Foundation Hashtags

1. #racedialogueusa
2. #racismdialogueusa
3. #atriskchildrenusa
4. #youthorganizingusa
5. #stopblackonblackusa
6. #newleadershipusa
7. #1619commemorationusa
8. #africanslaveryusa
9. #indigenouspeopleusa
10. #afrocentricusa
11. #civillibertiesusa
12. #civilrightsusa
13. #humanrightsusa
14. #saveourchildrenusa
15. #parentalschoolchoiceusa
16. #wearyourmaskusa
17. #defeatcovid19usa
18. #socialdistanceusa
19. #racismapublichealthcrisis

Printed in the United States
By Bookmasters